MICHIGAN STATE UNIVERSITY

JOSH ANDERSON

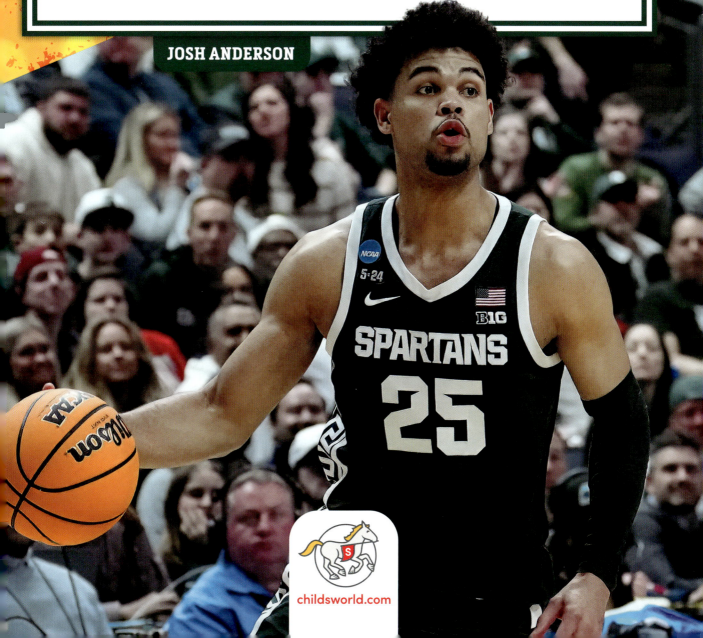

childsworld.com

Published by The Child's World®
800-599-READ • www.childsworld.com

Copyright © 2024 by The Child's World®
All rights reserved. No part of this book may be reproduced or utilized in any form or by any means without written permission from the publisher.

Photography Credits
page 1: ©Dylan Buell/Stringer/Getty Images; page 2: ©Mitchell Layton/Contributor / Getty Images; page 5: ©Bettmann/Contributor/Getty Images; page 7: ©Bettmann/Contributor/Getty Images; page 8: ©David C Azor/Shutterstock; page 9: ©Andy Lyons/Staff/Getty Images; page 11: ©Gregory Shamus/Stringer/Getty Images; page 12: ©NCAA Photos/Contributor/Getty Images; page 15: ©Jed Jacobsohn/Staff/Getty Images; page 16: ©Matthew Holst/Contributor/Getty Images; page 17: ©Bettmann/Contributor/Getty Images; page 18: ©Icon Sports Wire/Contributor/Getty Images; page 21: ©NCAA Photos/Contributor/Getty Images; page 23: ©Gary Mook/Stringer/Getty Images; page 24: ©Aaron J. Thornton/Contributor/Getty Images; page 27: ©Jamie Schwaberow/Contributor/Getty Images; page 28: ©Justin Ford/Stringer/Getty Images

ISBN Information
9781503885240 (Reinforced Library Binding)
9781503885462 (Portable Document Format)
9781503886100 (Online Multi-user eBook)
9781503886742 (Electronic Publication)

LCCN 2023937603

Printed in the United States of America

ABOUT THE AUTHOR

Josh Anderson lives in the Los Angeles area with his two sons and a giant dog. He's been to tons of sporting events, but his favorite was seeing sumo wrestling in Tokyo, Japan.

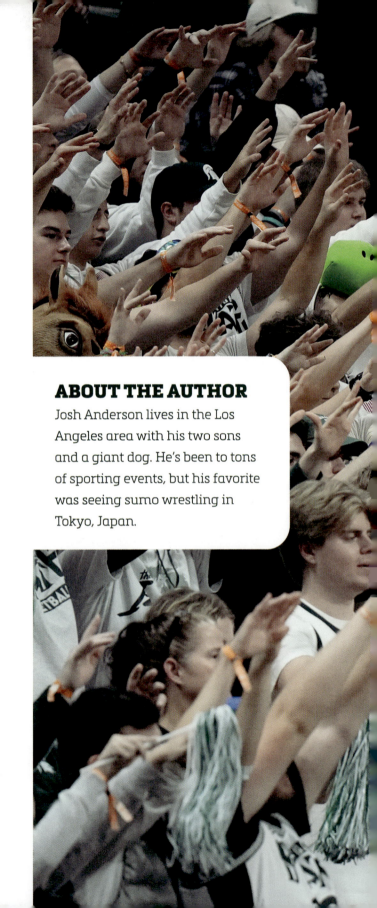

CONTENTS

CHAPTER ONE
Origins . . . 4

CHAPTER TWO
Rivalries . . . 10

CHAPTER THREE
Great Moments . . . 14

CHAPTER FOUR
All-Time Greats . . . 20

CHAPTER FIVE
The Modern Era . . . 26

Glossary . . . 30
Fun Facts . . . 31
One Stride Further . . . 31
Find Out More . . . 32
Index . . . 32

CHAPTER ONE

Origins

Michigan State University first opened its doors in 1857 in East Lansing, Michigan. When it started, the school was called the Agricultural College of the State of Michigan, and 63 students were enrolled. It became Michigan State College in 1925, and then Michigan State University in 1964. Nearly 50,000 students study there now.

Michigan State's teams are called the Spartans. Spartans were powerful warriors in ancient Greece. Michigan State's mascot is a Greek warrior wearing a helmet. His name is Sparty.

Michigan State's men's basketball program started in 1899 and joined the **NCAA**'s Big Ten **Conference** in 1949. The team's first big success was in 1957. That year, Michigan State played in the **NCAA Tournament** for the first time. The Spartans lost to the University of North Carolina Tar Heels in the **Final Four**.

Michigan State's Pete Gent (right) grabs a rebound in a 1963 game against the University of Pennsylvania.

Led by superstar Earvin "Magic" Johnson, the Spartans won their first national championship in 1979. Tom Izzo took over as the team's head coach in 1995. Izzo has led the Spartans to the NCAA Tournament in 25 of his 28 seasons on the sidelines. Under Izzo, Michigan State won its second national title in 2000. The team last played in the Final Four in 2019.

Michigan State University Spartans

TEAM NAME: Michigan State Spartans

FIRST SEASON: 1899 (Men's Team); 1972 (Women's Team)

CONFERENCE: Big Ten Conference

CONFERENCE CHAMPIONSHIPS: 16 (Men's Team); 4 (Women's Team)

HOME ARENA: Breslin Student Events Center

NCAA TOURNAMENT APPEARANCES: 36 (Men's Team); 18 (Women's Team)

NATIONAL CHAMPIONSHIPS: 2 (Men's Team); 0 (Women's Team)

Before his legendary NBA career, Earvin "Magic" Johnson played two seasons for the Spartans.

ORIGIN OF TEAM NAME

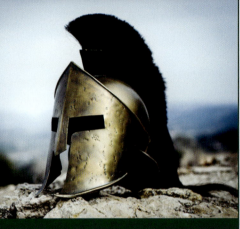

In its early days, Michigan State's teams were called the Aggies after the school's original name. In 1925, they held a contest to name the school's teams. The winning name was the Michigan Staters. A local sports journalist disliked the name. He looked at the other contest entries and began using Spartans when writing about the team. The name stuck.

Women's basketball began at Michigan State in 1972 and joined the Big Ten in 1982. Karen Langeland was the team's head coach from 1976 until 2000. Langeland led Michigan State to the NCAA Tournament for the first time ever in 1991. The team's best season was in 2004–05. Coach Joanne Palombo-McCallie led the Spartans to a 33–4 record. The team made it all the way to the national championship game but lost 84–62 to Baylor University. The Spartans' women's team last earned a trip to the NCAA Tournament in 2021.

The Big Ten is one of the best conferences in all of college basketball. Year after year, the Spartans try to compete for the conference title and a chance to play in the NCAA Tournament. While it doesn't always go Michigan State's way, the school is always a top team in both men's and women's basketball.

Michigan State's Liz Shimek tries to find a teammate for a pass during the Spartans' Final Four matchup with Tennessee in 2005.

CHAPTER TWO

Rivalries

Rivals are teams who have a long history of playing each other for the right to claim they are the best. Michigan State's biggest rival is the University of Michigan Wolverines. The Wolverines also compete in the Big Ten Conference. Because the schools are in the same conference, they play at least twice every season. Since both schools are often at the top of the Big Ten, they sometimes play a third time in the conference tournament.

Michigan State's men's basketball team first played the Wolverines in 1909. The Spartans won the game 24–16. Michigan has won 97 of the 185 games between the two teams. In 2019, the teams met up in the finals of the Big Ten Conference tournament for only the second time ever. Michigan State had won the regular season title over the Wolverines by one game. Both teams were ranked in the top 10 in the country.

Adreian Payne, who played for the Spartans from 2010 to 2014, dunks against rival Michigan.

Early in the second half, the Wolverines held a 39–26 lead. It looked like Michigan might cruise to the victory. But the Spartans roared back.

Michigan still led 65–60 with just over two minutes remaining in the game. Michigan State guard Matt McQuaid made a huge three-pointer. McQuaid scored a career-high 27 points in the game, including 7 three-pointers. With 29 seconds remaining and the game tied 60–60, point guard Cassius Winston put the Spartans up for good with a layup. The Spartans won the game 65–60. Since 2019, the Spartans have won 7 of their 11 games against the Wolverines.

Michigan State's women's team played the Wolverines for the first time in 1973. Michigan State won the game 61–24. One of the most memorable games between the two teams was in the 2014 Big Ten Tournament. Michigan State tied for the regular-season conference title that year. The team was confident they'd advance to the NCAA Tournament. But the Wolverines were tough. They finished the season with an 18–13 overall record.

For most of the game, it looked like the underdog Wolverines would defeat the Spartans. Their lead was up to 14 points during the first half. But with just a little more than a minute left to play, the Spartans turned it around.

Spartans guard Tori Jankoska hit a layup to put Michigan State up 59–58. Then, after a Michigan turnover, Michigan State scored again. The Spartans held on until the buzzer and won 61–58.

Michigan State has won 73 of the 98 games between the two schools. But recent meetings have turned the tide. The Wolverines have beaten the Spartans in six of their seven games since 2020. The Spartans are hopeful that their dominance over the Wolverines will return in the years to come.

First Meeting:
1909 (Men's Teams); 1973 (Women's Teams)

Michigan State's Record against Michigan:
88–97 (Men's); 73–25 (Women's)

CHAPTER THREE

Great Moments

Michigan State women's basketball had its best season ever in 2004–05. The Spartans finished 13–3 in the conference and won the Big Ten title. They ended the season with a 33–4 overall record. All-Big Ten guard Kristin Haynie led the conference in **assists** and steals.

The Spartans beat the Stanford Cardinal to earn a trip to the Final Four for the first time in school history. They played the Tennessee Volunteers, who were led by coaching legend Pat Summitt.

After Tennessee took a 31–25 lead into halftime, they came out even stronger in the second half. Tennessee was ahead 16 with about 14 minutes to go in the game. It looked like the Spartans' dream season was close to ending.

But the Spartans cut the lead little by little until they finally tied the score with about a minute remaining in the game. Haynie had only scored two points in the game but stole the ball and dribbled in for a layup.

The Spartans had plenty to celebrate in 2005 when they made it all the way to the national championship game of the NCAA Tournament.

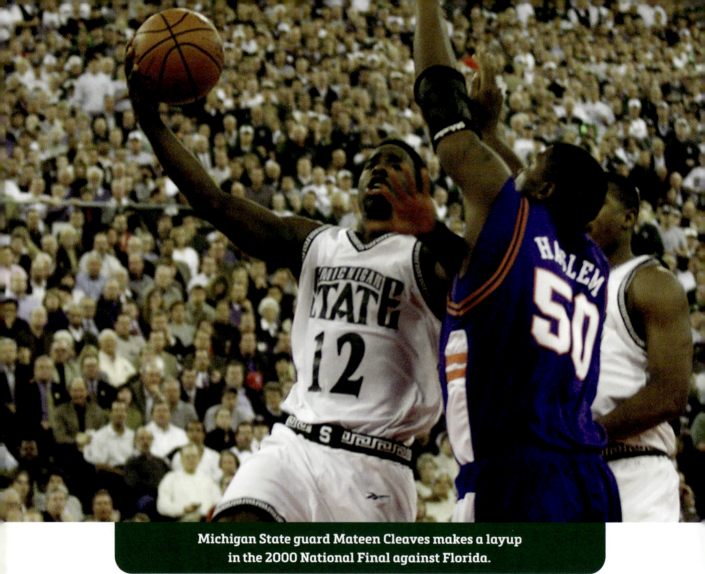

Michigan State guard Mateen Cleaves makes a layup in the 2000 National Final against Florida.

Her basket put the Spartans ahead. Michigan State stopped Tennessee from scoring for the remainder of the game. The Spartans won the game 68–64 in one of the greatest comebacks in NCAA Tournament history. Although they lost the final game to Baylor University, the 2004–05 season was an incredible one for Michigan State women's basketball.

Michigan State's men's team has won two NCAA Championships. The most recent was in 2000. Led by two-time Big Ten Player of the Year Mateen Cleaves, the Spartans won every NCAA Tournament game by double digits. While coach Tom Izzo has led the team to the Final Four six times since then, the Spartans have been without a national title since their incredible 2000 run.

Michigan State won its first NCAA title in one of college basketball's most memorable games. Not only did Michigan State win the Big Ten in 1978–79, but it also had one of the most exciting players in the history of the sport. Magic Johnson played his second and final season of college basketball that year. He went on to be picked first in the 1979 NBA **Draft**. Magic and the Spartans were matched up in the final game of the NCAA Tournament against the Indiana State Sycamores.

THAT'S STRANGE!

Unfortunately, the 2022–23 Michigan State Spartans' men's team proved that anything is possible in college basketball. The Spartans led the Iowa Hawkeyes in a late-season game. The score was 91–78 with just over a minute left to play. In the game's final 90 seconds, Iowa hit 6 three-pointers and scored 23 points to tie the score 101–101. The game went into overtime, and the Spartans lost 112–106.

Before their famous NBA rivalry, Magic Johnson (left) and Larry Bird (center) battled in the 1979 National Championship game.

The Sycamores had never played in the NCAA Tournament. But they had that season's National Player of the Year, Larry Bird. They also had a perfect 33-0 record coming into the final against the Spartans.

While both Johnson and Bird led their teams in scoring, the Spartans led for most of the game. Michigan State took the title by a score of 75-64.

Bird and Johnson continued their rivalry for many years in the NBA. Their meeting in the 1979 Championship game is considered the beginning of one of the most important rivalries in sports history. The game also helped college basketball become more popular in the United States.

CHAPTER FOUR

All-Time Greats

Tori Jankoska's incredible senior year in 2016–17 sent her to the top of the Michigan State women's career **rankings** in several categories. She averaged 22.6 points per game as a senior, the most in school history. She graduated as the Spartans' all-time leading scorer with 2,212 points. Jankoska is also Michigan State's all-time leader with 320 three-point field goals and ranks third with 489 assists. Jankoska led the Spartans to one Big Ten title and three NCAA Tournament appearances during her four seasons at Michigan State.

Guard Shawn Respert played for the Spartans from 1990 to 1995. He's Michigan State's all-time leading scorer with 2,531 points. He also ranks second in scoring in Big Ten history. Respert is also the Spartans' career leader with 331 three-point field goals. He was named an All-American in 1994 and 1995. As a senior, Respert averaged 25.6 points per game.

Spartans guard Tori Jankoska pulls down a rebound during a game against Maryland.

THE G.O.A.T.

Magic Johnson is Michigan State's all-time leader in **triple-doubles** with eight. He doesn't rank at the top of many other Spartans career leader boards because he only played two seasons at the school. But Magic changed the game of basketball. Before he played, point guards were not usually top scorers or rebounders. Magic showed that point guards could score, rebound, and control their team's offense. He also played with a flair not often seen from a six-foot-eight (203.2 centimeters) player. Johnson went on to a Hall of Fame pro career, leading the Los Angeles Lakers to five NBA titles.

Respert helped lead Michigan State to the NCAA Tournament three times in his career. The team retired his number 24 jersey in 1998. No Michigan State player will wear that number in the future.

Liz Shimek was a key player on the Spartans' team that played in the 2005 Final Four. Shimek played for Michigan State from 2002 to 2006 and finished her career as the Spartans' all-time leader in rebounds with 1,130. Her 443 offensive rebounds rank fourth in Big Ten Conference history. Shimek also ranks fifth in Spartans' history with 108 blocked shots. She was picked for the 2005–06 All-Big Ten Team.

Tom Izzo is one of the greatest college basketball coaches in the history of the sport. He took over as head coach of the Spartans in 1995 and remains the team's coach today. Izzo has led the Spartans to 25 NCAA Tournaments in a row.

Known as one of the best passers of all time, Magic Johnson always had his eyes peeled for an open teammate.

Under Izzo, Michigan State has won the Big Ten Conference title 10 times and been to the Final Four 8 times. He coached the team to the national title in 2000. The National Association of Basketball Coaches has named Izzo Coach of the Year twice.

Mateen Cleaves was the top player on the Spartans' 2000 National Championship team. He was named an All-American three times and the Big Ten's Player of the Year twice. Cleaves ranks second in Michigan State history and Big Ten Conference history with 816 career assists. His 195 steals are the most in school history. He also holds the school record for most steals in a single game. Cleaves had nine in a 1998 game against the University of Minnesota.

◀ **The school's all-time leading scorer, Shawn Respert, goes for a layup in a game against Purdue University.**

CHAPTER FIVE

The Modern Era

The Michigan State women's team struggled in 2022–23. Coach Suzy Merchant has led the Spartans to 4 Big Ten titles and 10 NCAA Tournament appearances in her 16 seasons in East Lansing. But Michigan State hasn't been to the tournament since 2021 when it lost in the first round. After top scorer Kamaria McDaniel and top rebounder Taiyier Parks graduated in 2023, the program started rebuilding with younger players.

The Spartans' men's team finished the 2022–23 season with a trip to the NCAA Tournament for the 25th season in a row. The Spartans were fourth in the Big Ten with an 11–8 record and advanced to the **Sweet 16** in the NCAA Tournament before losing to Kansas State 98–93. Guard Tyson Walker and forward Joey Hauser provided great scoring for the Spartans, but both graduated in 2023. Izzo started his 29th season as Michigan State's coach in 2023–24.

Guard Kamaria McDaniel averaged more than 14 points per game as a senior in 2022–23.

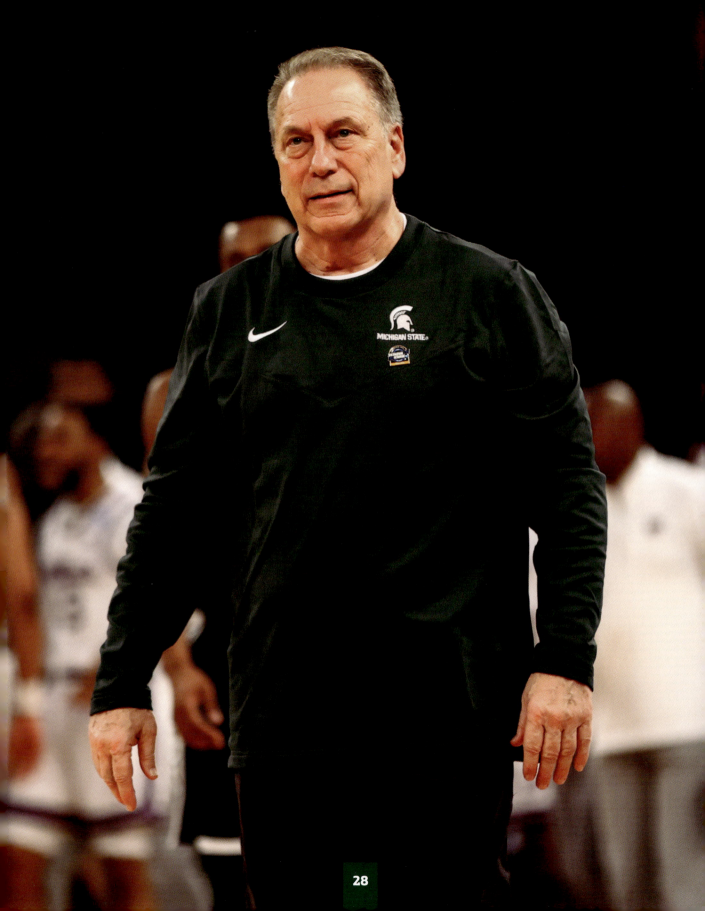

Michigan State's 25 straight NCAA Tournament appearances are the second-longest active streak in college basketball. Izzo is looking to keep that streak going. But no matter what the future holds, Michigan State fans will come to games and cheer loudly for the Spartans.

TEARING UP THE LEAGUE!

Jaren Jackson Jr. was named the Big Ten's Rookie of the Year and Defensive Player of the Year after his one season at Michigan State in 2017–18. The Memphis Grizzlies picked Jackson fourth in the 2018 NBA Draft. He led the NBA in blocked shots during the 2021–22 season and was named to the NBA's All-Defensive Team. Jackson was an All-Star for the first time in 2022–23.

◀ Head coach Tom Izzo has led the Spartans to 687 wins since taking over in 1995.

GLOSSARY

All-Star (ALL STAR) a player chosen as one of the best in a league, such as the NBA or WNBA

assists (uh-SISTS) passes that lead directly to a basket

conference (KON-fuhr-enss) a group of teams that compete and play against each other every season

draft (DRAFT) a yearly event when the best amateur players are picked by professional teams

Final Four (FY-null FOR) games between the top four teams in the NCAA Tournament

NCAA (National Collegiate Athletic Association) a group that oversees college sports in the United States

NCAA Tournament (TUR-nuh-mint) a competition between 68 teams at the end of the college basketball season that decides the national champion

rankings (RANK-ingz) a list of individuals or teams that have achieved high numbers in a statistical category

Sweet 16 (SWEET six-TEEN) games between the top 16 teams in the NCAA Tournament

triple-doubles (TRIH-puhl DUH-buhlz) games in which a player accumulates 10 or more in 3 statistical categories (example: points, rebounds, and assists)

FUN FACTS

- Nia Clouden, who played for the Spartans from 2018 to 2022, was picked 12th overall in the 2022 WNBA Draft by the Connecticut Sun.

- Spartans all-time leading scorer Shawn Respert led Michigan State in scoring all four years he played for the team. He's the only Spartan men's player ever to do so.

- Allyssa DeHaan played for the Spartans from 2006 to 2010. Her 503 blocked shots rank third all-time in women's college basketball history.

- Terry Furlow scored the most points ever in a single game with 50 in a 1976 game against Iowa.

- Only three men's basketball teams have longer streaks than the Spartans' 25 straight appearances in the NCAA Tournament.

ONE STRIDE FURTHER

- Michigan State's men's team has been consistently successful, making 25 NCAA Tournaments in a row. Think about what role consistency plays in your own life. What things do you make sure to do each and every day to make yourself the happiest and the most successful? Are there other things you don't do consistently but wish you did?

- Make a list of your favorite college basketball players. Include two things about each player that make them your favorite. Is it the way they play? Their attitude on the court? What else?

- Ask your friends and family members about their favorite sport. Keep track, and make a graph to see which sport wins out.

FIND OUT MORE

IN THE LIBRARY

Berglund, Bruce. *Basketball GOATs: The Greatest Athletes of All Time*. New York, NY: Sports Illustrated Kids, 2022.

Buckley, Jr., James. *It's a Numbers Game! Basketball*. Washington, DC: National Geographic Kids, 2020.

Stabler, David. *Stephen Curry vs. Magic Johnson: Who Would Win?* Minneapolis, MN: Lerner Publications, 2023.

Williamson, Ryan. *College Basketball Hot Streaks*. Mankato, MN: The Child's World, 2020.

ON THE WEB

Visit our website for links about Michigan State University basketball:
childsworld.com/links

Note to Parents, Caregivers, Teachers, and Librarians: We routinely verify our web links to make sure they are safe and active sites. So encourage your readers to check them out!

INDEX

Big Ten Conference, 4, 6, 8, 10, 12, 14, 17, 20, 22, 25–26, 29

Cleaves, Mateen, 16–17, 25

East Lansing, Michigan, 4, 26

Hauser, Joey, 26
Haynie, Kristin, 14

Izzo, Tom, 6, 17, 22, 25–26, 29

Jankoska, Tori, 13, 20–21
Johnson, Earvin "Magic", 6, 17–19, 22

Langeland, Karen, 8

McDaniel, Kamaria, 26–27
McQuaid, Matt, 12
Merchant, Suzy, 26

Parks, Taiyier, 26

Respert, Shawn, 20, 22, 25, 31

Shimek, Liz, 9, 22

Walker, Tyson, 26
Winston, Cassius, 12